KANSAS CITY CHIEFS

JULIE NELSON

Published by Creative Education
123 South Broad Street, Mankato, Minnesota 56001
Creative Education is an imprint of The Creative Company

Designed by Rita Marshall

Photos by: Allsport USA, AP/Wide World Photos, Bettmann/CORBIS,
SportsChrome

Library of Congress Cataloging-in-Publication Data

Nelson, Julie.
Kansas City Chiefs / by Julie Nelson.
p. cm. — (NFL today)
Summary: Traces the history of the team from its beginnings through 1999.
ISBN 1-58341-047-3

1. Kansas City Chiefs (Football team)—History—Juvenile literature. [1. Kansas
City Chiefs (Football team)—History. 2. Football—History.] I. Title. II. Series:
NFL today (Mankato, Minn.)

GV956.K35N45   2000
796.332'64'0977844—dc21   99-015740

First edition

9 8 7 6 5 4 3 2 1

A long the Missouri River in the central United States are two Kansas Cities, situated right next to each other. The Kansas City in Missouri is located along the western edge of the state, while the Kansas City in Kansas is at the eastern edge of that state.

Kansas City, Missouri, is a bustling city of almost 450,000 citizens, making it nearly three times as big as its twin city on the other side of the river. For nearly 40 years, the Kansas City in Missouri has also been home to a professional football team that has captured three league championships—the Kansas City Chiefs.

Quarterback great Len Dawson.

Running back Abner Haynes was the AFL's first rushing champion, gaining 875 yards.

The Chiefs didn't start out in Kansas City, though. The team began playing in 1960 as the Dallas Texans, one of the original eight teams in the American Football League. The owner of the Texans, Lamar Hunt, was from Texas and wanted his team to play in his home state. But Hunt had a problem. In 1960, an older, more established league—the National Football League—started an expansion team called the Cowboys in Dallas. After the powerful NFL laid claim to the city of Dallas, Lamar Hunt was forced to look elsewhere for a home for his team.

FROM TEXANS TO CHIEFS

While Hunt looked for another city in which to settle his franchise, the Texans and their coach, Hank Stram, prepared to play the 1962 season. In training camp that year was Len Dawson, a quarterback who was looking to latch on to a new club after playing five years in the NFL. Dawson had been with the Pittsburgh Steelers and the Cleveland Browns, and he was considered a good player with a lot of potential. Both the Steelers and the Browns, however, had been unhappy with his throwing techniques and had cut him loose.

Stram believed that Dawson could still become a top-notch quarterback and offered to help him correct his bad throwing habits. The gamble paid off. With Dawson leading the way, the Texans rolled to an 11–3 record and won the Western Division of the AFL. Helping Dawson lead the offensive attack was halfback Abner Haynes, who scored a league-record 19 touchdowns.

Sure-handed tight end Tony Gonzalez.

1 9 6 6

Mike Garrett balanced the Chiefs' offense by rushing for 801 yards.

In the 1962 league championship game, the Texans beat their intrastate rivals, the Houston Oilers, 20–17 in sudden-death overtime. Dawson was named the AFL Player of the Year. Yet despite the Texans' success, Dallas fans did not support the team, giving their attention to the Cowboys instead. After the season, the Texans moved to Kansas City and became the Chiefs.

The change of scenery also changed the team's luck, though not in a positive way. The Texans had finished as winners in Dallas, but the Chiefs would not start out that way. Kansas City wound up third in the Western Division in 1963 with a 5–7–2 record.

OTIS TAYLOR AND SUPER BOWL GLORY

The Chiefs improved to 7–7 the following year, but they were still far from their previous championship form. They needed more weapons, and in 1965, they found one in Otis Taylor, a wide receiver with a world of talent.

What made Taylor special was his size and strength. At 6-foot-3 and 215 pounds, he was huge by wide receiver standards of the time. "Some receivers have great speed and great moves," Dawson explained. "Otis has both, plus size and strength."

Taylor knew exactly how good he was. "I'll tell you something about Otis Taylor," he once said. "He wants to be the best—always. There hasn't been a year when he didn't want to score more touchdowns than anybody and gain more yardage than anybody. At the start of the season, I aim for the top 10 and higher. And I don't quit."

8

The Chiefs didn't quit in 1966 until they had won the Western Division and defeated the Buffalo Bills in the league championship game. In previous years, the season had ended after the AFL title game. But in 1966, the AFL champion Chiefs played the NFL champs, the Green Bay Packers, in a game called the AFL-NFL Championship Game. Lamar Hunt didn't like that name. "Why don't we just call it the Super Bowl?" he suggested. The name would stick.

Few people gave the Chiefs much of a chance against the powerful Packers. But the fans were clearly curious about this new championship game. More than 65 million people watched the game on television—the largest single audience for an athletic event in the history of television.

1 9 7 0

Scrappy halfback Ed Podolak charged for a team-high 749 yards and scored four touchdowns.

After Green Bay struck first, the Chiefs scored a touchdown of their own, tying the game 7–7 in the second quarter on Dawson's seven-yard pass to fullback Curtis McClinton. But behind quarterback Bart Starr, the Packers would run away to a 35–10 victory.

The experts saw the Chiefs' loss as proof that the older NFL was clearly a better league than the AFL. But in 1968, the New York Jets shocked the football world. The Jets, champs of the AFL, defeated the NFL champion Baltimore Colts 16–7 in Super Bowl III. Still, most fans called it a fluke. The next season, in 1969, Kansas City went 13–3 and won the AFL championship.

The Chiefs' opponent in Super Bowl IV would be the Minnesota Vikings. The oddsmakers set the Vikings as 13-point favorites, but the Chiefs weren't impressed. This was a different Kansas City team than the one that had lost in Super Bowl I.

Two former defensive stars: cornerback Dale Carter . . .

. . . and linebacker Tracy Simien.

Wide receiver Otis Taylor caught 57 passes for 1,110 total yards.

Soon, though, a major distraction arose. A couple of days before the Super Bowl, a newspaper report surfaced that linked Dawson to professional gamblers. The Kansas City quarterback was accused of betting money on pro football games, including those played by the Chiefs. If proven true, the charges could have led to a lifetime ban from football. Even though the allegations were quickly dropped, the rumors bothered Dawson and angered his teammates. The Chiefs were more ready than ever.

Kansas City dominated the Vikings in the first half, with three long drives all ending in Jan Stenerud field goals. Late in the half, Dawson drove Kansas City to the Vikings' five-yard line. On third down, Minnesota's defenders braced for a pass. Dawson rolled out to his right before handing the ball to Mike Garrett, who ran back to the left and into the end zone. The Vikings, behind 16–0, were stunned.

In the second half, the Vikings scored a touchdown early in the third quarter and appeared to steal the momentum. But Dawson and the Chiefs responded to the challenge. From the Vikings' 46-yard line, Dawson faded back and threw a sideline pass to Taylor. Although it was a short-yardage play designed to get a first down and little more, Taylor had other ideas, breaking two hard tackles before scoring to give the Chiefs a 23–7 lead. Dawson knew the game was over. "That was the touchdown I wanted," Dawson said. "I knew we had them. . . . I could sense the frustrations of the Minnesota defense. They weren't able to do the things they had been doing all year against the NFL teams."

The game ended at 23–7. The Chiefs had destroyed a team that was supposed to win by two touchdowns. Dawson, who was named the Player of the Game, had performed almost flawlessly, completing 12 of 17 passes. In the locker room after the game, Dawson explained the Chiefs' success against the best defense in football. "Our game plan really wasn't very complicated," Dawson said. "It involved throwing a lot of formations at them—formations they hadn't seen during the course of the season."

When the NFL and AFL merged into one league in 1970, the Chiefs were placed in the Western Division of the American Football Conference along with the Oakland Raiders, Denver Broncos, and San Diego Chargers. Oakland won the AFC West in 1970, but Kansas City took the division title in 1971, earning the right to host the Miami Dolphins in the first round of the playoffs. The contest took place on Christ-

1 9 7 2

Hall of Fame tackle Buck Buchanan led the Chiefs for the 10th season.

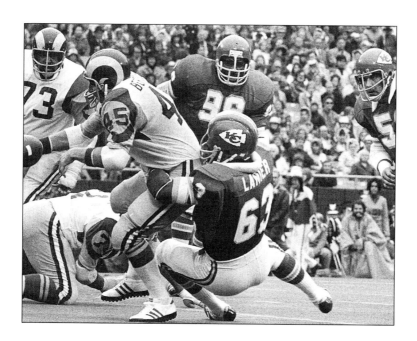

One of the game's most ferocious tacklers, Willie Lanier.

1 9 7 9

Kicker Jan Stenerud played the final season of his 13-year Kansas City career.

mas Day, but the long, hard-fought battle left players and fans feeling as though a winner wouldn't be decided until after the New Year.

Dawson had hit Elmo Wright on a 63-yard touchdown pass to give the Chiefs a 24–17 lead in the fourth quarter. Miami tied the score with 90 seconds left. Dawson then drove Kansas City into field-goal range, but the usually reliable Jan Stenerud missed the kick, sending the game into sudden-death overtime.

Both Stenerud and Dolphins kicker Garo Yepremian had chances to kick the game winner in the extra quarter, but both missed. For only the second time in pro football history, the game went into a sixth quarter. Yepremian got another chance midway through the second overtime. His kick split the uprights, and the Dolphins won 27–24. To this day, no NFL game has lasted longer than the 82 minutes and 40 seconds that the Chiefs and Dolphins battled.

The game was the last ever played in Kansas City's Municipal Stadium. Unfortunately for the Chiefs, the game was also the last postseason game the team would play for 15 years. In 1972, the Chiefs moved to the new Arrowhead Stadium, a gorgeous arena with almost 80,000 seats—30,000 more than Municipal Stadium had.

Although the Chiefs posted winning records in 1972 and 1973, they missed the playoffs each time. After a 5–9 season in 1974, Coach Stram was fired. A year later, both Dawson and Taylor retired. Despite the efforts of such standouts as defensive end Art Still and linebacker Gary Spani, the team slid to the bottom of the AFC West in the late 1970s and stayed there for several years.

Crafty quarterback Steve DeBerg.

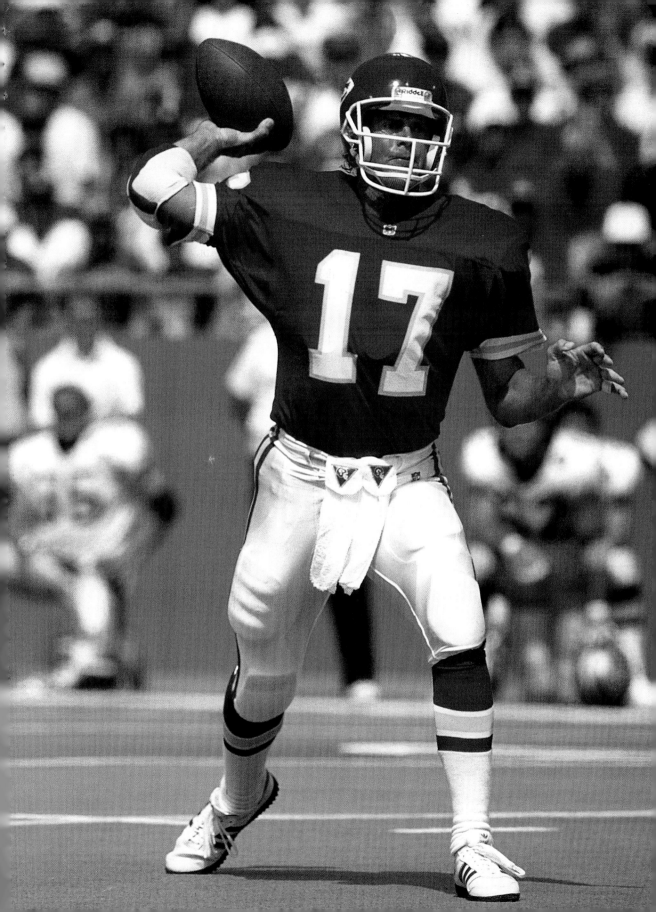

Cornerback Albert Lewis combined concentration and speed.

THE JOE DELANEY TRAGEDY

The Chiefs struggled until 1980, when new coach Marv Levy brought the team back to respectability. Kansas City finished 8–8 that season and expected bigger things in 1981. The addition of a rookie running back named Joe Delaney in 1981 made Kansas City one of the most improved teams in the NFL. Delaney was small, but he had quick feet and great speed. In his rookie year, Delaney gained 1,121 rushing yards, a Kansas City team record, and was named AFC Rookie of the Year.

Behind Delaney's brilliance, the Chiefs went 9–7 and nearly made the playoffs in 1981, but late-season injuries and inconsistency at the quarterback position crushed the team's chances. The following year, a players' strike wiped out almost half of the season. Still, Delaney had another solid season and established himself as one of the best backs in the game. But on June 29, 1983, on a hot day in Monroe, Louisiana, all of that changed.

On that day, Delaney was on the shore of a lake playing catch with some friends. Suddenly, he heard cries for help. A panicked little boy ran up to Delaney and told him that three other boys were drowning. "I can't swim good, but I've got to save those kids," Delaney told his friends. "If I don't come up, get somebody." Delaney then jumped into the lake to try to save the boys.

One of the boys managed to make it to shore, but two of them—and Joe Delaney—didn't make it back. In only a matter of minutes, one of pro football's brightest young stars was gone, dead at the age of 24.

1 9 8 1

Rookie halfback Joe Delaney racked up a combined 1,367 yards on runs and pass receptions.

The "Nigerian Nightmare," Christian Okoye (pages 18-19).

"People ask me, 'How could Joe have gone in the water the way he did?'" said Delaney's college coach, A.L. Williams. "And I answer, 'Why, he never gave it a second thought, because helping people was a conditioned reflex to Joe Delaney.'"

After Joe Delaney's death, the Chiefs slipped to last place in the AFC West the next season. Levy was fired and replaced by John Mackovic, who built a winning team led by quarterback Bill Kenney and an excellent defense that featured perhaps the finest secondary in the NFL. Safeties Deron Cherry and Lloyd Burruss and cornerbacks Albert Lewis and Kevin Ross made life miserable for opposing quarterbacks and wide receivers.

The improved Chiefs made the playoffs in 1986 but lost in the first round to the New York Jets. Despite the postseason appearance, Mackovic was fired. New head man Frank Gansz replaced Mackovic, but the Chiefs slumped again.

1 9 8 7

Defensive end Art Still left Kansas City after making 992 career tackles.

THE "NIGERIAN NIGHTMARE"

In Coach Gansz's first year, the Chiefs found a gem in the 1987 NFL draft: a 6-foot-3 and 260-pound bruiser of a running back named Christian Okoye. Okoye grew up in Nigeria and came to the United States on a track scholarship, only to discover the strange new game of football while attending Azusa Pacific University.

A couple of years later, the Chiefs had themselves a Nigerian fullback whom Azusa track coach Terry Franson called "one of the best big athletes in the world." In 1989, new coach Marty Schottenheimer decided the Chiefs had to give

Okoye the ball more—a lot more. Okoye responded by leading the NFL in rushing, bulling his way for 1,480 yards and 12 touchdowns.

"I can remember Marty asking me, 'How many times do you think you can carry the ball in a game?'" Okoye reflected. "I told him I once carried 40 times in college. I told him I often carried 30 times a game at Azusa. Marty was surprised I told him I could do that. It is no problem for me."

Okoye impressed his offensive linemen as well as Schottenheimer. "To feel the force he runs with is amazing," said tackle Irv Eatman. "He has slammed into my back on running plays a few times, and the only way I can describe what it feels like is to imagine standing on the street and getting hit by a car going 50 miles an hour."

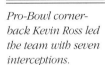

Pro-Bowl corner-back Kevin Ross led the team with seven interceptions.

Wideout Stephone Paige helped Okoye lead the offense. 21

Defensive end Neil Smith was an explosive pass rusher.

Although Okoye was known as a gentle and soft-spoken man away from the football field, he was a terror when he lined up in the backfield. The "Nigerian Nightmare," as he was called, pulverized defenses and struck fear in the hearts of would-be tacklers. His hard running sounded a warning to the rest of the AFC West—the Chiefs were on their way up once again.

PLAYOFF STREAKING IN THE '90s

In the 1990s, the Chiefs established themselves under Schottenheimer's steady hand as perennial contenders. Kansas City made it to the playoffs six straight years from 1990 to 1995—the longest streak by any NFL team in the decade. The Chiefs' success bore out the simple philosophy of their head coach. "The best way to establish a position of excellence in the NFL," Schottenheimer once explained, "is to expect it." Schottenheimer expected nothing less, and his players did not let him down.

In 1990, young linebacker Derrick Thomas put together one of the greatest years ever by a defensive player. He not only led the league with 20 sacks, but he also set an NFL record by sacking the quarterback seven times in a single game against the Seattle Seahawks. Veteran quarterback Steve DeBerg led the Chiefs' offense, which featured powerful runner Barry Word as a new threat to accompany Okoye in the backfield. The Chiefs finished 11–5 in 1990 but fell to Miami in the first round of the playoffs.

The following year, the Chiefs went one step further by recording their first playoff win in 22 years, defeating the Los

1 9 9 2

Head coach Marty Schottenheimer led the Chiefs to a third straight season with at least 10 victories.

Veteran runner Marcus Allen found his way into the end zone 12 times.

Angeles Raiders 10–6 in a hard-fought Wild Card game. But Schottenheimer was convinced that the offense needed strengthening. In 1992, free agent quarterback Dave Krieg, a former Seattle Seahawks standout, led the Chiefs to another winning season. In the first round of the playoffs, however, the Chiefs were shut down by the San Diego Chargers, 17–0. Schottenheimer then decided to go one big step further in his search for a Super Bowl-caliber quarterback: he would acquire a legend.

Joe Montana had led the San Francisco 49ers to four Super Bowl victories. In three of those Super Bowls, Montana was named the game's Most Valuable Player. But Montana sat out nearly all of the 1991 and 1992 seasons with an elbow injury, and the 49ers decided to make Steve Young

The great Joe Montana.

their quarterback of the future. The Chiefs, believing that Montana could regain his superstar form, traded for the future Hall-of-Famer.

Montana repaid Kansas City for its faith in him. In 1993, he was named AFC Offensive Player of the Week four times while leading Kansas City to an 11–5 record and its first division championship in 22 years. Montana didn't do it all alone, however. Just before the season started, the Chiefs also acquired free agent running back Marcus Allen, a long-time star with the Raiders who had ridden the bench in recent seasons. With Kansas City, Allen proved that his skills were still intact by rushing for 764 yards and balancing Montana's precision passing attack. The Chiefs made it all the way to the AFC championship game before falling to the Buffalo Bills, 30–13.

Montana retired after the 1994 season, but Schottenheimer and the Chiefs continued their winning ways. Their new starting quarterback, Steve Bono, had been Montana's backup in San Francisco. Bono ably guided the Chiefs to a 13–3 regular-season record in 1995—the best in the NFL—with the help of Marcus Allen, who ran for 890 yards. Meanwhile, the team's defense, led by Pro-Bowlers Derrick Thomas, cornerback Dale Carter, and end Neil Smith, dominated opposing offenses, giving up seven or fewer points in five games.

In the first round of the playoffs, however, Kansas City was upset by the Indianapolis Colts, and Coach Schottenheimer faced criticism about his failure to make it to the Super Bowl. Still, he remained proud of his team's achievements and confident that a Super Bowl was within reach.

1 9 9 5

Neil Smith led Kansas City in quarterback sacks (12) for the third straight season.

Dominant linebacker Derrick Thomas (pages 26-27).

1 9 9 7

Fullback Kimble Anders's 59 receptions led all AFC running backs.

Pride was all the Chiefs had in 1996, as they finished 9–7 but failed to make the playoffs for the first time in seven seasons. Most experts overlooked Kansas City the following season, calling 1997 a rebuilding year. Pro-Bowl defensive end Neil Smith had signed with Denver in the off-season, and the defense, though feisty, was young and inexperienced. The Chiefs featured 11 new starters, four of them rookies on the defensive side.

The Chiefs defied all predictions by roaring out of the gates in 1997. With a stifling defense, Kansas City went undefeated at home, finishing the season with a 13–3 record and its third AFC West title in five years. Quarterbacks Elvis Grbac and Rich Gannon split time at the quarterback position, firing downfield to their favorite target: new arrival Andre Rison.

Rison, who had spent eight seasons with five different teams before joining Kansas City, hoped to resurrect his career, vowing to "give Kansas City the best wide receiver in the NFL and repay the Chiefs for giving [him] a second chance." Working hard to be true to his word, in 1997 the flamboyant receiver gave the Chiefs 72 catches and 1,092 receiving yards. Rison quickly became a fan favorite in Kansas City, adopting the nickname "Spider-Man" because of his sure hands and the team's red uniforms. Unfortunately, Spider-Man and the Chiefs couldn't get past the Broncos in the first round of the playoffs, falling 14–10.

Just as no one expected the Chiefs to dominate in 1997, few fans could have predicted that the following season would be the team's worst in a decade. What was supposed to be a Super Bowl season for Kansas City turned into a nightmare. Dependable back Marcus Allen retired before the season, and the Chiefs lacked a dominant presence at running back. Many other players were bothered by injuries.

Though the Chiefs started the 1998 season 4–1, cracks soon began to appear in their armor. Grbac struggled at quarterback and was eventually replaced by backup Rich Gannon. The Chiefs lost six straight games in the middle of the season. Near the end of that dismal streak, the franchise hit a new low point.

All-Pro guard Will Shields anchored the Chiefs' line for the seventh season.

On November 16, the Chiefs hosted rival Denver. Late in the game, trailing 27–7, frustration finally got the best of the Kansas City defense. In a nine-play Denver scoring drive, Chiefs defenders committed five personal fouls, including late quarterback hits and blatant face mask violations.

As a result of the breakdown, the Chiefs cut linebacker Wayne Simmons and dealt Derrick Thomas a one-game suspension. But the damage had been done. Over the course of the season, Kansas City amassed an NFL-record 158 penalties. The Chiefs limped to a final 7–9 record—the first losing season of Schottenheimer's 15-year coaching career. Schottenheimer retired after the season, ending a Chiefs coaching career that encompassed a 101–58–1 final record and three AFC West titles.

Schottenheimer's successor was Chiefs defensive coordinator Gunther Cunningham, a 17-year NFL assistant coach known for his motivational skills. Cunningham and the Chiefs took off-season steps to change their fortunes in 1999 by implementing a shotgun formation and reinstating quarterback

Linebacker Donnie Edwards excelled against the run.

Accurate passer Elvis Grbac.

2 0 0 1

Chiefs fans counted on tight end Tony Gonzalez to power the team's offense.

Elvis Grbac as the team's starter. "I think we have tremendous players here," announced Coach Cunningham. "We can be explosive on offense."

Grbac proved his coach right by throwing for 3,389 yards and 22 touchdowns. Many of Grbac's passes went to end Tony Gonzalez and receiver Derrick Alexander, who combined for 1,681 receiving yards. The team's strongest point, however, may have been its defense, perhaps the most punishing in all of football.

In the last game of the season, the 9–6 Chiefs needed to beat Oakland to make the playoffs. With just seconds left and the game tied 38–38, kicker Pete Stoyanovich had a chance to win the game for Kansas City, but his long field goal attempt sailed wide. In overtime, the Raiders struck first, eliminating the Chiefs from the playoffs. Although the loss was painful, it paled in comparison to the tragedy that struck a month later.

Derrick Thomas, the team's all-time sacks leader and one of the most dominant players of the '90s, crashed his car while driving in snowy conditions. One of his passengers was killed, and two weeks later, Thomas died as well. Football fans across the nation mourned the loss of a legendary player and a great man. "He had so much love for the game, for his teammates, and for our town," said Chiefs team president Carl Peterson. "A light has gone out."

As they begin a new century of football, the Chiefs hope to honor their fallen leader by forging ahead to further glory. For four decades, Kansas City has carved out a winning tradition in America's heartland, and today's Chiefs look more than ready to continue that tradition.

32